CAREER ANCHORS

PARTICIPANT WORKBOOK

THIRD EDITION

Edgar H. Schein

Pfeiffer
A Wiley Imprint
www.pfeiffer.com

ISBN-10: 0-7879-7759-4
ISBN-13: 978-0-7879-7759-7

Acquiring Editor: Lisa Shannon
Director of Development: Kathleen Dolan Davies
Developmental Editor: Susan Rachmeler
Production Editor: Dawn Kilgore
Editor: Rebecca Taff
Manufacturing Supervisor: Becky Carreño

Printed in the United States of America
Printing   10   9   8   7   6   5   4   3   2

Contents

Introduction

THE PURPOSE OF THIS WORKBOOK is to give you information about career development, to provide you with a process that will enable you to assess more fully your career anchor, and to provide you with a process for analyzing your current job situation as well as possible future career options. To improve the career development process, you must understand fully how careers develop, what role career anchors play in that development, and how career anchors relate to job characteristics.

The *Career Anchors Self-Assessment* that you completed to give yourself an initial picture of your career orientations should now be supplemented by exploring more fully how career anchors develop, how different anchors function, and how they relate to job situations. To gain more insight into your own situation, this workbook provides you with instructions to do a personal career history, either by yourself in written form or, preferably, with the help of another person who would interview you and provide some feedback. (See pages 28–33.)

The second exercise, called Job/Role Analysis and Planning (pages 39–43), will help you to analyze your present career and job situation, provide some guidance on how to think about the future world of work, help you to assess your strengths and weaknesses in terms of future job requirements, and will enable you to determine what you need to do next for your own personal development.

Career Development

The "Internal Career" and Career Anchors

The word "career" is used in many different ways and has many connotations. Sometimes "having a career" is used to apply only to someone who has a profession or whose occupational life is well structured and involves steady advancement. But if we think of a career as being what *any* individual would regard as the steps and phases of his or her occupation, then everyone has a career, and that career is "anchored" by the person's self-image of his or her competencies, motives, and values.

One might consider this to be the "internal career," to distinguish it from what others might view that person's work life to be. Everyone has some kind of picture of his or her work life and role in that life. To distinguish the "internal career" from other uses of the word, we will use "external career" to refer to the actual steps that are required by an occupation or an organization to progress through that occupation. A physician must complete medical school, internship, residency, specialty board examinations, and so on. In some organizations, a general manager has to go through several business functions, have experience in supervising people, take on a functional management job, rotate through the international division, and serve on the corporate staff before being given a true generalist job as a division general manager. Most external careers involve a period of training or apprenticeship during which the person both learns and is tested to determine whether he or she has the skills and personal characteristics to do the job. Some organizations talk of career paths, which define the necessary or at least desirable steps for the career occupant to take along the way to some goal job. The clearest example of that kind of formal path is probably the military, with its well-defined ranks and clear rules for how one goes from one rank to another.

At the other extreme is what more and more people are calling a "boundaryless" career or a "protean" career that is more free-form, has to be managed more by the career occupant, and may involve movements across many employers (Arthur & Rousseau, 1996; Hall, 2002). Whereas organizations used to promise "employment security," employers are increasingly promising nothing at all or only *"employability* security," implying that you will learn on-the-job skills that will make you more employable *elsewhere.*

It is this trend toward having to manage your own career more and more, even if you are in a single organization, that makes it more important than ever to understand your internal career and the role that career anchors play in it.

External Career Stages and Career Movement

Externally defined career stages are usually well defined by formal occupational criteria and by organizations if the career is embedded in an organization. Thus, a young engineer can pretty well see his or her external career in terms of the amount of schooling necessary, entry into an organization as a technical person or management trainee, followed by that organization's specification of how it defines "career development." Most organizations have some career "paths" that are based on historical data of what previous entrants have experienced and can tell the young engineer or manager to be what steps to expect. However, the career world is changing, and there are fewer and fewer standard paths visible in occupations and organizations.

What one can analyze by viewing a large number of organizations and occupations is certain generic career stages: (1) a period of pre-career choosing of a field and educational preparation for entry into that field; (2) formal training in the chosen field or occupation; (3) entry into the occupation or organization; (4) a period of learning, apprenticeship, and socialization; (5) a period of full use of one's talent, leading to some form of granting of tenure through being given permanent membership, a professional license, or some other form of certification; (6) a period of productive employment; (7) a branching into administrative, managerial, and other forms of becoming a "leader"; (8) gradual disengagement, part-time work, and eventual retirement.

At any point in the external career, the person may discover that his or her internal career and career anchors are out of line with what the external career offers in terms of challenge, opportunities, and rewards. At that point, the person may switch to another career and start going through the stages over again, but usually in a more truncated form because the experience acquired in one career is often transferable to another career. The engineer employed in a technical organization may discover a talent and desire for entrepreneurial work or for management and may decide to start a company or switch to an organization that provides more managerial opportunities. Some training in management may then be required, and the person may have to start at the bottom of a new career ladder.

Career stages in the external career can be thought of as a series of movements along three different dimensions: (1) moving *up* in the hierarchical structure of the occupation or organization; (2) moving *laterally* across the various subfields of an occupation or functional groups of an organization; and (3) moving *in* toward the centers of influence and leadership in the occupation or organization. Depending on what the person is looking for in his or her internal career, movement along each of these dimensions will have different meanings. For some, such as managers, it is *moving up* that is important; for some, such as the technical person, it is job challenge and *lateral movement* to new and challenging work that is most important; and for some, such as the power or socially motivated person, it is *moving toward the inner circle* and positions of influence that is most important. People with different career anchors will seek movement in different dimensions. Figure 1 helps to illustrate these three dimensions.

Each dimension has its own stages associated with it, but these are usually idiosyncratic in particular occupations or organizations. In summary, career stages in the externally defined career are the sequence of roles and statuses defined by a particular occupation or organization as the way to progress through the career. They may or may not correspond to the individual's own sense of his or her internal career stages.

Development of the Career Anchor in the Internal Career

With each educational or job experience, we have an opportunity to learn. It is important to go beyond just *judging* each experience as good or bad, fun or not, useful or not, and to ask, "What have I learned about myself?" As we grow, we need not only to learn what is "out there" in the arena of work, but also what our own reactions are to the experiences. These reactions are best thought of in terms of three domains:

1. *Skills and competencies.* You need to learn from each experience what you are good at; that learning comes both from your own assessment and from the feedback you receive from others;

2. *Motives.* You need to learn from each experience what it is you really desire; early in life we think we know what we want, what our career aspirations are, but with each experience we discover that there are things we like or don't like, that some of our aspirations are unrealistic, and that we develop new ambitions.

3. *Values.* You need to learn from each experience what it is you value in the context of what your occupation or organization considers important, what your colleagues value, and how the kind of organizational climate you encounter fits with those values.

As you gain experience, you become more clear about each of these domains until you have a self-concept of what you are good at and not good at, want and do not want, and value or do not value. This self-concept is your *career anchor.*

The self-concept builds on whatever self-insight you have acquired from the experiences of youth and education. However, it cannot be a mature self-concept until you have had enough real *occupational* experience to know what your talents, motives, and

Figure 1. A Three-Dimensional Model of an Organization*

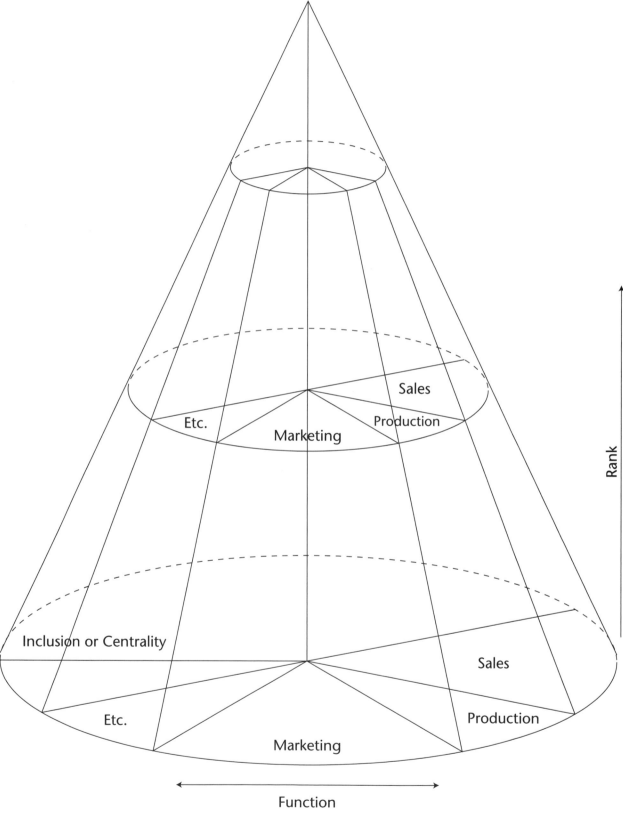

*From "The Individual, the Organization, and the Career: A Conceptual Scheme," by E.H. Schein, 1971, *Journal of Applied Behavioral Science, 7,* p. 404. Copyright 1971 by JAI Press, Inc. Reprinted by permission.

values are. Such learning may require up to ten years or more of actual work experience. If you have had many varied experiences and have received meaningful feedback with each one, your self-concept will have developed more quickly. But if you have had only a few jobs in the early years of your career and/or have obtained minimal feedback, it may take much longer.

Talents, motives, and values become intertwined so it may be hard to figure out what your anchor is. People learn to be better at those things they value and are motivated to do; and they learn to value and become motivated by those things they happen to do well. They also gradually learn to avoid those things that they do not do well, although, without clear feedback, they may cling to illusions about themselves that set them up for repeated failures. Talents without motivation gradually atrophy. Conversely, new challenges can reveal latent or hidden talents that simply had not had an opportunity to appear earlier.

People differ initially as to whether it is their talents, their motives, or their values that dictate their early career choices. As time goes on, however, a need for congruence causes people to seek consistency and integration among these different elements of their self-concepts. How is this consistency learned? People first enter the world of work with many ambitions, hopes, fears, and illusions but with relatively little good information about themselves, especially about their abilities and talents. Through testing and counseling, they gain an idea of their interests, motives, and values as well as their intellectual and motor skills, but they cannot really determine how good they will be at a certain kind of work or how they will react to it emotionally.

Nowhere is this more true than in moving from a technical job into a supervisory and managerial role because of the difficulty in simulating during the educational period some of the interpersonal and emotional skills needed in those roles. Until a person actually feels the responsibility of committing large sums of money, of hiring and firing people, of saying "no" to a valued subordinate, that person cannot tell whether he or she will be able to do it or will like doing it. In many occupations, a person cannot tell whether he or she has the talent or the emotional makeup to do the job without actually performing that job.

For these reasons, the early years in an occupation are a crucial time of learning—learning about the occupation or organization and learning about oneself in relation to the demands of the job. This process is often painful and full of surprises because of the many misconceptions and illusions with which people typically enter their early work situations. Many of the dreams people have for themselves about what their work will be like may be inconsistent with their work experiences, causing "reality shock," a phenomenon that is observed in all occupations in the early years.

As you accumulate work experience, you have the opportunity to make choices; from these choices you begin to ascertain what you really find important. Dominant themes emerge—critical skills or abilities that you want to exercise or crucial needs or values that dominate your orientation toward life. You may have had a vague sense of these elements but, in the absence of actual life experience, you do not know how important they are or how any given talent, motive, or value relates in a subjective hierarchy to other elements of your total personality. Only when you are confronted with difficult choices do you begin to decide what is really important to you.

With accumulation of work experience and feedback come clarification and insight, providing a basis for more rational and empowered career decisions. The self-concept begins to function more and more as a guidance system and as an anchor that constrains career choices. You begin to have a sense of what is "you" and what is "not you." This knowledge keeps you on course or in a safe harbor. As people recount their career choices, they increasingly refer to "being pulled back" to things they have strayed from or "figuring out what they really want to do" or "finding themselves." This process leads people to gradually move from having broad goals to a sense of knowing better what it is that they would not give up if forced to make a choice. The career anchor, as defined here, is that one element in a person's self-concept that he or she will not give up, even in the face of difficult choices. And if their work does not permit expression of the anchor, people find ways of expressing it in their hobbies, in second jobs, or in leisure activities.

The Eight Career Anchor Categories

THE EIGHT CAREER ANCHOR CATEGORIES that are reviewed below were originally discovered in longitudinal research and subsequently confirmed in a variety of studies of different occupations and in different countries (Schein, 1971, 1975, 1977, 1978):

- Technical/Functional Competence (TF)
- General Managerial Competence (GM)
- Autonomy/Independence (AU)
- Security/Stability (SE)
- Entrepreneurial Creativity (EC)
- Service/Dedication to a Cause (SV)
- Pure Challenge (CH)
- Lifestyle (LS)

They were briefly reviewed in the Self-Assessment booklet and are explored more fully here.

Several other categories of career concerns have been proposed, but none have shown up consistently as "anchors," as the one thing the person would not give up. For example, "variety," "status or identity," and "power" have been proposed as additional anchors but have not shown up consistently in research, hence are not included in the orientation questionnaire. When you look at these categories, you will realize that every person is "concerned" to some degree with each of these issues. And most occupations make it possible to fulfill needs in several of those areas. But they are probably not equally important to you, so it is important to know their relative strength in you, and what you would not give up if forced to make a choice.

To understand this concept fully and to determine your own anchor, you need to look at each of the anchors in greater detail and to understand how people with different anchors differ from one another. The following descriptions of the eight anchors are intended to provide you with this information. Each description begins with the general characteristics of the anchor and then examines the developmental issues involved, such as the type of work, pay and benefits, growth opportunities, and recognition preferred by a person with that career anchor.

Technical/Functional Competence

Some people discover as their careers unfold that they have both a strong talent and high motivation for a particular kind of work. What really "turns them on" is the exercise of their talents and the satisfaction of knowing that they are experts. This can happen in any kind of work. For example, an engineer may discover that he or she is very good at design; a salesperson may find real selling talent and desire; a manufacturing manager may encounter greater and greater pleasure in running complex plants; a financial analyst may uncover talent and enjoyment in solving complex capital investment problems; a teacher may enjoy his or her growing expertise in the field; and so on.

As these people move along in their careers, they notice that if they are moved into other areas of work they are less satisfied and less skilled. They begin to feel "pulled back" to their areas of competence and enjoyment. They build a sense of identity around the *content* of their work, the technical or functional areas in which they are succeeding, and develop increasing skills in those areas.

The technically/functionally anchored commit themselves to a life of specialization and devalue the concerns of the general manager, although they are willing to be *functional* managers if it enables them to pursue their areas of expertise. Most careers start out being technical/functional in their orientation, and the early phase of many organizational careers is involved with the development of a specialty, but not everyone is excited by a specialty. For some people, the specialist job is a means to organizational membership or security more than it is an end in itself. For others, it is simply a stepping stone to higher rungs on the organizational ladder, a necessary step to move into general management. For still others, it is an opportunity to learn some skills that will be needed to launch into independent or entrepreneurial activities. Consequently, although most people start out specializing, only some find this *intrinsically* rewarding enough to develop career anchors around their specialties.

Preferred Type of Work

The single most important characteristic of desirable work for members of this group is that it be challenging to them. If the work does not test their abilities and skills, it quickly becomes boring and demeaning and will result in their seeking other assignments. Because their self-esteem hinges on exercising their talent, they need tasks that permit such exercise. Although others might be more concerned about the *context* of the work, this type of person is more concerned about the intrinsic *content* of the work.

Technical/functional people who have committed themselves to an organization (as opposed to being an autonomous consultant or craft person) are willing and anxious to share in goal setting. However, once goals have been agreed on, they demand maximum autonomy in executing them. Not only do they want the autonomy in execution, but they generally also want unrestricted facilities, budgets, and resources of all kinds to enable them to perform the job appropriately. Conflict often emerges between general managers who are trying to limit the cost of specialized functions and the specialists who want to be able to spend whatever it takes to enable them to do the job properly as they see it.

The person anchored in this way will tolerate administrative or managerial work as long as he or she believes that it is essential to getting the job done; however, such work is viewed as painful and necessary, rather than as intrinsically enjoyable or desirable. Being promoted into a more general job is viewed as totally undesirable because it forces them out of the specialties with which they identify.

Talent for the interpersonal aspects of management varies in this group, resulting in the dilemma that, if such people are promoted into supervisory positions and then discover that they have no talent for supervision, they are typically blocked organizationally. Most career ladders do not provide for easy return to the technical/functional staff role once a managerial job has been taken.

Finding a viable role and challenging work as one progresses in a technical/functional career can be a difficult task, both for the individual and for the organization. Becoming more of a teacher and mentor to younger people is one workable solution. Careful redesign of work to take advantage of the experience level of the older specialist is another avenue, inasmuch as this kind of person becomes something of a generalist within his or her technical area and is thus able to bring a broader perspective to problems.

Preferred Form of Pay and Benefits

Technical/functional people want to be paid for their skill levels, usually defined by level of education and work experience. A person with a doctorate wants a higher salary than someone with a master's degree, regardless of actual accomplishments. These people are oriented toward *external equity,* meaning that they will compare their salaries to what others of the same skill level earn in *other* organizations. Even if they are the highest-paid people in their own organizations, they will feel that they are not being treated fairly if they are underpaid compared with those in similar positions in other organizations.

Technical/functional people are oriented more toward absolute pay level than toward special incentives such as bonuses or stock options, except as forms of recognition. They probably prefer so-called "cafeteria" portable benefits, in which they choose the kinds of benefits they need (for instance, life insurance or retirement programs) because they view themselves as highly mobile and want to be able to take as much as possible with them. They are frightened of the "golden handcuffs" because they might become trapped in unchallenging work.

Preferred Growth Opportunities

Moving ahead in this group is measured by the increasing technical challenge that is provided by new job assignments. "Promotion" is also measured by increasing autonomy and support for educational opportunities. This group of people clearly prefers a professional or technical promotional ladder that functions in parallel with the typical managerial ladder. They resent promotional systems that make advancement equivalent to moving into administration or management. Functional ladders have been utilized primarily in some research-and-development and engineering organizations, but they are just as applicable to all the other functional specialties that exist in organizations (such as finance, marketing, manufacturing, or sales). Still, very few organizations have developed career ladders that are genuinely responsive to the growth needs of the technically/functionally anchored person.

Growth for a technically/functionally anchored person does not have to be a promotion in terms of rank. If external market equity is achieved in salary, this person would respond to being awarded an increase in the scope of the job, to being allocated more resources or areas of responsibility, to being given a bigger budget or more technical support or subordinates, or to being consulted more on high-level decisions as a result of placement on key committees or task forces.

Preferred Type of Recognition

The specialist values the recognition of his or her professional peers more than uninformed rewards from members of management. In other words, a pat on the back from a supervisor who really does not understand what was accomplished is worth less than acknowledgment from a professional peer or even from a subordinate who knows exactly what was accomplished and how difficult it might have been.

In terms of the type of recognition that is valued, at the top of the list is the opportunity for further learning and self-development in the specialty. Thus, educational opportunities, organization-sponsored sabbaticals, encouragement to attend professional meetings, budgets for buying books or equipment, and so on are highly valued. This is especially true because one of the greatest threats to technically/functionally anchored people as they age is obsolescence.

In addition to continuing education, this group values formal recognition through being identified to colleagues and other organization members as valued specialists. Prizes, awards, publicity, and other public acknowledgments are more important than an extra percentage in the paycheck, provided that the base pay is perceived as equitable in the first place.

The technically/functionally anchored person is most vulnerable to organizational mismanagement because organizational careers tend to be designed by general managers who value quite different things, as we will see below. In summary, in terms of career movement, this kind of person wants to climb only a technical ladder and become more influential in his or her organization, but would and should resist either cross-functional movement or the general management ladder.

General Managerial Competence

Some people—but only some—discover as their careers progress that they really want to become general managers, that management per se interests them, that they have the range of competencies that are required to be a general manager, and that they have the ambition to rise to organizational levels at which they will be responsible for major policy decisions and their own efforts will make the difference between success and failure of the organization.

Members of this group differ from the technical/functional people in that they view specialization as a trap, even though they recognize the necessity to know several functional areas well and accept that one must be expert in one's business or industry to function well in a general manager's job. Key values and motives for this group of people are advancement up the corporate ladder to higher levels of responsibility, opportunities for leadership, contributions to the success of their organizations, and high income.

When they first enter organizations, most people have aspirations to get ahead in some general sense. Many of them talk explicitly of ambitions to rise to the top, but few have a realistic picture of what is actually required in the way of talents, motives, and values to make it to the top. With experience, it becomes clearer to them that they not only need a high level of motivation to reach the top, but that they also need a mixture of talents and skills in the following three basic areas:

Analytical Competence

Analytical competence is the ability to identify, to analyze, to synthesize, and to solve problems under conditions of incomplete information and uncertainty. General managers continually point out the importance of being able to decipher what is going on; to cut through a mass of possibly irrelevant detail to get to the heart of a matter; to judge the reliability and validity of information in the absence of clear verification opportunities; and, in the end, to pose the problem or question in such a way that it can be worked on. Financial, marketing, technological, human, and other elements have to be combined into problem statements that are relevant to the future success of the organization.

It is commonly said that general managers are *decision makers*. However, it is probably more accurate to say that general managers are capable of identifying and stating problems in such a way that decisions can be made. General managers manage the decision-making *process*; to do this, they must be able to think cross-functionally and integratively. That, in turn, requires other competencies.

Interpersonal and Intergroup Competence

This type of competence is the ability to influence, supervise, lead, handle, and control people at all levels of the organization toward organizational goal achievement. General managers point out that this skill involves eliciting valid information from others, being able to hear and act on information coming from below, getting others to collaborate to achieve synergistic outcomes, motivating people to contribute what they know to the problem-solving process, communicating clearly the goals to be achieved, facilitating the decision-making process and decision implementation, monitoring progress, and instituting corrective action if necessary.

Much of the technical information that goes into decision making increasingly is in the hands of subordinates and peers with technical/functional career anchors. Therefore, the quality of decisions largely hinges on the ability of general managers to bring the right people together for problem-solving purposes and then to create a climate that will elicit full exchange of information and full commitment from these people. As organizations become more technically complex and global, they also become more multicultural, which means that general managers must create the conditions for cross-cultural communication and dialogue. More and more decision making will occur in multifunctional and multicultural groups because the complexity of the problems requiring more sophisticated group skills. As problems become more complex, so do the rewards of integrating the many agendas and approaches into a coherent strategy and successfully implementing it.

New managers often wonder whether they will be any good at supervising others and, of almost equal importance, whether they will *like* supervising and managing complex group situations. Most new managers do not know what interpersonal skills they have or need unless they have been in leadership roles in school. This is one reason why management recruiters are anxious to know about extracurricular activities when they assess candidates for general manager jobs. Any evidence of a track record in this area is of great value, both to the individual and to the organization. Once a new manager has had an opportunity to test himself or herself and finds that the interpersonal work is manageable and enjoyable, self-confidence and ambition increase rapidly.

People who discover either that they are not talented in supervision or that they do not really like that kind of work gravitate toward other pursuits and build their career anchor around technical/functional competence, autonomy, or even entrepreneurial activity. It is crucial for organizations to create career systems that make it possible for such people to move out of supervisory roles if they are not suited to such roles, preferably without penalty. All too often the best engineer or salesperson is promoted to be a supervisor, only to fail in the role, but then is stuck in it, to the inevitable detriment of his or her career and the effectiveness of the organization.

Emotional Competence

Emotional competence encompasses the capacity to be stimulated by emotional and interpersonal issues and crises, rather than to be exhausted or debilitated by them; the capacity to bear high levels of responsibility without becoming paralyzed; and the ability to exercise power and make difficult decisions without guilt or shame. General managers who are interviewed about their work refer to the painful process of learning to make "tough" decisions, and almost all of them say that they had not anticipated what it would be like or how they would react. Only as they gained confidence in their abilities to handle their own feelings did they gain confidence that they could really succeed as general managers. They cited as examples such decisions as laying off a valued older employee; deciding between two programs, each backed by valued subordinates; committing large sums of money to a project, knowing that the fate of many people depended on success or failure; asking a subordinate to perform a very difficult job that he or she might not want to do; inspiring a demoralized organization; fighting for a project at a higher level; delegating to subordinates and leaving them alone enough to learn how to do things; shutting down a project that may leave hundreds or thousands out of a job; moving a plant out of a community knowing that it spells economic doom for that community; and taking ownership of a decision, in the sense of being accountable even without control over its implementation.

Most general managers report that such decisions must be made repeatedly and that one of the most difficult aspects of the job is functioning day after day, twenty-four hours a day, every day of the week, without giving up or having a nervous breakdown. The essence of the general manager's job is to absorb the emotional strains of uncertainty, interpersonal conflict, and responsibility. It is this aspect of the job that often repels the technically/functionally anchored individual but excites and motivates the managerially anchored individual.

General managers differ from people with other anchors, primarily in that they have a combination of analytical competence, interpersonal and intergroup competence, and emotional competence. They cannot function well without some degree of competence in each of these areas. It is the *combination* of skills that is essential for the general manager, while the technical/functional person can get along on high development of one skill element. General managers are quite different in these respects from functional managers, and it takes longer to learn to be a general manager because these competencies can only be learned through actual experiences.

Preferred Type of Work

People with a general management anchor want high levels of responsibility; challenging, varied, and integrative work; leadership opportunities; and opportunities to contribute to the success of their organizations. They will measure the attractiveness of a work assignment in terms of its importance to the success of the organization, and they will identify strongly with the organization and its success or failure as a measure of how well they have done. In a sense, then, they are real "organization people," whose identity rests on having an effective organization to manage. This sense of identity contrasts sharply with the T/F anchored person, whose identity derives from the professional or technical peer group *inside and outside* the organization.

Preferred Form of Pay and Benefits

Managerially anchored people measure themselves by their income levels and expect to be very highly paid. In contrast to technically/functionally anchored people, they are oriented more toward *internal* equity than external equity. They want to be paid substantially more than the level below them and will be satisfied if that condition is met, even if someone at their own level in another company is earning more. They also want short-term rewards, such as bonuses for achieving organizational targets, and, because they are identified with the organization, they are very responsive to things such as stock options that give them a sense of ownership and shared fate.

Managerially anchored people share with security-oriented people a willingness (if not a positive desire) for the "golden handcuffs," particularly in the form of good retirement benefits. So much of a managerially anchored person's career is tied up with a given company that his or her particular skills may not be portable in mid-life or later. However, an increasing number of general managers now shift from company to company and take their benefit packages with them or negotiate for equivalent packages. Inasmuch as intimate knowledge of a particular industry and company are important to the decision-making process, it is not clear whether such movement is or can be successful. It is possible that new specialties are arising within general management itself, such as the "turnaround manager," who is brought into a failing company from outside to get it back to a profitable status; the "start-up manager," whose specialty is to open new parts of the organization in overseas locations or to develop new products or markets; or the "project manager," who is brought in to integrate many functions in a complex enterprise, such as developing a major weapons system or new aircraft or building an oil refinery.

Preferred Growth Opportunities

Managerially anchored people prefer promotion to a higher level or greater responsibility based on merit, measured performance, and results. Even though they acknowledge that personality, style, seniority, politics, and other factors play a role in determining promotions, general managers believe that the ability to obtain results is and should be the critical criterion. All other factors are legitimate only because they are essential to getting results.

Preferred Type of Recognition

The most important forms of recognition for managerially anchored people are promotions to positions of higher responsibility. They measure such positions by a combination of rank, title, salary, number of subordinates, and size of budget, as well as by less tangible factors defined by their superiors (such as the importance of a given project or department or division to the future of the company). They expect promotions frequently. If they are too long in a given job, they assume that they are not performing adequately or are not appreciated.

Every organization's culture develops explicit or implicit timetables for promotions, and managers measure their successes partly by whether they are moving in accordance with their organizations' timetables. Thus, movement itself becomes an important form of recognition, unless it is clearly lateral or downward. Organizations sometimes develop implicit career paths that become known informally to the more ambitious general managers. It may be commonly understood, for example, that one should move from finance to marketing, then take over a staff function in an overseas company, then move to headquarters, and eventually take over a division. If promotions do not follow the typical path, these people will worry that they are "off the fast track" and are losing their potential. For this reason, movement to the right job is another important form of recognition.

This group of people is highly responsive to status symbols such as large offices, cars, or special privileges, and, most importantly, the approval of their superiors. Whereas the technically/functionally anchored person only values approval from someone who really understands his or her work, general managers value approval specifically from the superiors who control their most important incentive—promotion to the next-higher level. In summary, the person who is anchored in general managerial competence and who therefore aspires to a position in general management has a very different orientation from others in the organization, even though he or she may start in a very similar kind of job. Such an orientation develops as soon as the person has acquired enough data to determine whether or not he or she has the analytical, interpersonal, and emotional skills to be a general manager. Some people have these insights early. If the organization does not respond to their needs to rise quickly, they will seek out other organizations that permit them to reach responsible levels more rapidly.

Autonomy/Independence

Some people discover early in their working lives that they cannot stand to be bound by other people's rules, procedures, working hours, dress codes, and other norms that almost invariably arise in any kind of organization. Regardless of what they work on, such people have an overriding need to do things in their own way, at their own pace, and against their own standards. They find organizational life to be restrictive, irrational, and intrusive into their private lives; therefore, they prefer to pursue more independent careers on their own terms or organizational jobs that provide maximum freedom, such as being a salesman out in the field. If forced to make a choice between a present job that permits autonomy and a much better job that requires giving it up, the autonomy/independence-anchored person would stay in his or her present job.

Everyone has some need for autonomy, and this need varies during the course of life. For some people, however, this need comes to be overriding; they feel that they must be masters of their own ship at all times. Sometimes extreme autonomy needs result from being an only child or from high levels of education and professionalism, where the educational process itself teaches the person to be totally self-reliant and responsible, as is the case for many doctors and professors. Sometimes such feelings are developed in childhood by child-rearing methods that put great emphasis on self-reliance and independent judgment.

People who begin to organize their careers around such needs gravitate toward autonomous professions. If interested in business or management, they may go into consulting or teaching. Or they may end up in areas of work in which autonomy is relatively possible even in large organizations, such as research and development, field sales offices, data processing, market research, financial analysis, or the management of geographically remote units.

Preferred Type of Work

The autonomy-anchored person prefers clearly delineated, time-bounded kinds of work within his or her area of expertise. Contract or project work, whether part-time, full-time, or even temporary, is acceptable and often desirable. In addition, this type of person wants work that clearly defines goals but leaves the means of accomplishment up to him or her. The autonomy-anchored person cannot stand close supervision; he or she might agree to organization-imposed goals or targets but wants to be left alone after those goals are set.

Preferred Form of Pay and Benefits

The autonomy-anchored person is terrified of the "golden handcuffs." He or she would prefer merit pay for performance, immediate payoffs, bonuses, and other forms of compensation with no strings attached. People anchored in autonomy prefer portable, cafeteria-style benefits that permit them to select the options most suitable to their life situations at given points in time.

Preferred Growth Opportunities

This type of person responds most to promotions that reflect past accomplishments; he or she wants a new job to have even more freedom than the previous one. In other words, promotion must provide *more* autonomy. However, being given more rank or responsibility can threaten an autonomy-anchored person if it entails loss of autonomy. An autonomous sales representative knows that to become sales manager might mean less freedom, so he or she often turns down such promotions. A professor knows that becoming a department chair or dean means less freedom and may therefore elect to remain a professor.

Preferred Type of Recognition

The autonomy-anchored person responds best to forms of recognition that are portable. Medals, testimonials, letters of commendation, prizes, awards, and other such rewards probably mean more than promotions, title changes, or even financial bonuses.

Most organizational reward systems are not at all geared to dealing with the autonomy-anchored person. Hence such people often leave in disgust, complaining about organizational red tape. If their talents are not needed, no harm is done. But if key people in the organization such as computer programmers, financial analysts, or field sales representatives have autonomy anchors, it becomes important to redesign personnel systems to make organizational life more palatable to them. Such redesign is particularly difficult because most systems are not geared for dealing with contract or part-time work, the form of work that is often the most attractive to the autonomy-anchored person.

Security/Stability

Some people have an overriding need to organize their careers so that they feel safe and secure, so that future events are predictable, and so that they can relax in the knowledge that they have "made it." Everyone needs some degree of security and stability throughout life, and at certain life stages financial security can become the overriding issue, such as when one is raising and educating a family or approaching retirement. However, for some people, security and stability are predominant throughout their careers to the point that these concerns guide and constrain all major career decisions.

Security/stability-anchored people often seek jobs in organizations that provide job tenure, that have the reputation of avoiding layoffs, that have good retirement plans and benefit programs, and that have the image of being strong and reliable. For this reason, government and civil service jobs are often attractive to these people.

Security/stability-anchored people welcome the "golden handcuffs" and are usually willing to give responsibility for their career management to their employers. They obtain some of their satisfaction from identifying with their organizations, even if they do not have high-ranking or important jobs. In exchange for "tenure" they are willing to be told what work to do, how much to travel, where to live, how often to switch assignments, and so on. Because of this, they are sometimes perceived as lacking ambition or may be looked on with disdain in cultures that place a high value on ambition and achievement. This stereotype can be unfair because some of these individuals have risen from humble origins into fairly high-level managerial positions. When they reach middle management in large corporations, they genuinely feel they have made it because of where they started socioeconomically. The highly talented among this group reach high levels in organizations, but they prefer jobs that require steady, predictable performance. The less talented may level off in middle management or in staff jobs and gradually become less involved.

Preferred Type of Work

Security/stability-anchored people prefer stable, predictable work and are more concerned about the context of the work than the nature of the work itself. Job enrichment, job challenge, and other intrinsic motivational tools matter less to them than improved pay, pleasant working conditions, and benefits. Much organizational work has this character, and every organization is highly dependent on having among its employees a large number of people anchored in security and in technical/functional competence.

Preferred Pay and Benefits

The person anchored in security/stability prefers to be paid in steadily predictable increments based on length of service. Such a person prefers benefit packages that emphasize generous insurance, medical and retirement programs. Stock options and other forms of golden handcuffs are preferable to bonuses or other forms of unpredictable pay.

Preferred Growth Opportunities

The security/stability-anchored person prefers a seniority-based promotion system and welcomes a published grade-and-rank system that spells out how long one must serve in any given grade before promotion can be expected. Obviously, this kind of person relishes a formal tenure system such as is found in schools and universities.

Preferred Type of Recognition

The security/stability-anchored person wants to be recognized for his or her loyalty and steady performance, preferably with reassurances of further stability and continued employment. Above all, this person needs to believe that loyalty makes a real contribution to the organization's performance. Most personnel systems are well geared to this kind of person, although guarantees of tenure are becoming rare as organizations cope with growing complexity and globalization. For this reason, it is the security-anchored person who is most vulnerable as the external career systems are shifting away from employment security toward shorter-term contracts or even temporary employment.

Entrepreneurial Creativity

Some people discover early in life that they have an overriding need to *create* new ventures of their own by developing new products or services, by building new organizations through financial manipulation, or by taking over existing businesses and reshaping them to their own specifications. Creativity in some form or other exists in all of the career anchor groups, but what distinguishes the entrepreneur is that creating a new venture of some sort is viewed as essential to the career and to self-fulfillment. Inventors or artists or researchers also depend heavily on creativity, but they usually do not become committed to building new ventures around their creations. The creative urge in this anchor group is specifically toward creating new organizations, products, or services that can be identified closely with the entrepreneur's own efforts, that will survive on their own, and that will be economically successful. Making money is then one key measure of success.

Many people dream about forming their own businesses and express those dreams at various stages of their careers. In some cases, these dreams express needs for autonomy—to get out on one's own. However, entrepreneurially anchored people typically pursue such dreams relentlessly and early in life, often having started small money-making enterprises even during high school. They found they had both the talent and an extraordinarily high level of motivation to prove to the world that they could do it.

It is important to distinguish this career anchor from the autonomy/independence one. Many people want to run their own businesses because of autonomy needs and may fulfill those needs by buying small businesses, which they then run. What distinguishes entrepreneurs is their obsession with proving that they can *create* businesses. Such creation often means sacrificing both autonomy and stability, particularly in the early stages before a business is successful. Entrepreneurially anchored people often fail in their early efforts but keep searching for opportunities to try again and again. They may hold conventional jobs while planning their next efforts and even build their enterprises "on the side."

For example, a person may be a sales representative or a middle manager in some organization while trying to build a real-estate empire or looking for a company to acquire and run in his or her spare time. What makes such a person an "entrepreneur" is the dedication to creating the new enterprise and the willingness to drop a pre-existing job once a venture has been located.

Preferred Type of Work

Entrepreneurially anchored people are obsessed with the need to create, and they tend to bore easily. In their own enterprises, they may continue to invent new products or services, or they may lose interest, sell these enterprises, and start new ones. They are restless and continually require new creative challenges. If they are employed in organizations while they are planning their own ventures, they require jobs that either give them enough autonomy to pursue their side ventures or train them for the future, such as would be the case of the engineer who learns enough about a given product in an employing organization to eventually go out on his own with some new version of that product.

Preferred Pay and Benefits

For this group of people, ownership is ultimately the most important issue. Often they do not pay themselves very well, but they retain control of their organizations' stock. If they develop new products, they want to own the patents. Large organizations that attempt to retain entrepreneurs often misunderstand the intensity of these needs. Unless given control of the new enterprise with patents and 51 percent of the stock, an entrepreneurially anchored person will not stay with an organization, even though it offers to invest in his or her enterprise. Entrepreneurs want to accumulate wealth, not so much for its own sake but as a way of showing the world what they have accomplished. Benefit packages are not a central issue to them.

Preferred Growth Opportunities

Entrepreneurs want career systems that permit them to be wherever they need to be at any given point during their careers. Most of them want to be the head of their organizations, but often the managerial duties that are involved do not fit their talents or desires. In particular, if their ventures are successful it often requires good general management, something that the entrepreneur might not be good at and might not like. They then want the power and the freedom to move into other roles they consider to be key and to meet their own needs, usually roles that permit them to continue to exercise creativity, such as head of research and development or chairman of the board. In some cases, they sell their organizations and start new ones to fulfill their creative needs.

Preferred Type of Recognition

Building fortunes and sizeable enterprises are two of the most important ways that members of this group achieve recognition. In addition, entrepreneurs are rather self-centered, seeking high personal visibility and public recognition. Often they display this quality by putting their own names on products or on their companies.

Sense of Service/Dedication to a Cause

Some people enter occupations because of central values that they want to embody in their work and careers. They are oriented more toward these values than toward their actual talents or the areas of competence involved. Their career decisions are based on the desire to improve the world in some fashion. People with this anchor are attracted to the helping professions such as medicine, nursing, social work, teaching, and the ministry and to the many non-profit organizations or NGOs. However, dedication to a cause clearly also characterizes some people in business management and in organizational careers. Some examples include the human resource specialist who works on affirmative action programs, the labor lawyer intent on improving labor-management relations, the research scientist working on a new drug, the scientist working for environmental protection, or the manager who chooses to go into public service in order to improve some aspect of society in general. Values such as working with people, serving humanity, saving the environment, and helping one's nation can be powerful anchors in one's career.

It is important to note, however, that the helping professions are also attractive to the other anchor groups discussed so far. One can be a technically expert social worker or lawyer, one can pursue a career in medicine or teaching for autonomy or security reasons, and each of these occupations affords opportunities for entrepreneurship and general management. In other words, one should not assume that all people in service-type jobs have service anchors.

Preferred Type of Work

Service-anchored people clearly want work that permits them to influence their employing organizations in the direction of their values. A good example of this kind of person is a professor of agriculture who left a tenured university position to accept a job as manager of environmental planning for a large mining company. He stated that he would continue to work for this company as long as he was allowed to do key environmental planning and to have the power to get things done.

Preferred Pay and Benefits

People anchored in sense of service or dedication to a cause want fair pay for their contributions and portable benefits because they have no a priori organizational loyalty. Money per se is not central to them but, like the technical/functional person, they are concerned about *external equity*, that is, being paid fairly in relation to what others in their field receive.

Preferred Growth Opportunities

For this group, more important than monetary rewards is a promotional system that recognizes the contribution of the service-anchored person and moves him or her into positions with more influence and the freedom to operate more autonomously. Rotational systems that move such persons into higher-ranking areas where their values become irrelevant are clearly undesirable, but professional ladders that provide higher rank and influence within their service-oriented field are desirable.

Preferred Type of Recognition

Service-anchored people want recognition and support, both from their professional peers and from their superiors; they want to feel that their values are shared by higher levels of management. Like the technically/functionally anchored, they appreciate opportunities for more education, support for attendance at professional meetings, awards and prizes, and public acclaim for their accomplishments.

Pure Challenge

Some people anchor their careers in the need to prove over and over again that they can conquer anything or anybody. They define success as overcoming impossible obstacles, solving unsolvable problems, or winning out over extremely tough opponents. As they progress, they seek ever-tougher challenges. For some, this takes the form of seeking jobs in which they face more and more difficult problems. However, these people are not technically/functionally anchored because they seem not to care in what area the problem occurs. Some high-level strategy/management consultants seem to fit this pattern in that they relish more and more difficult kinds of strategic assignments, no matter what the industry or the company.

For others, the challenge is defined in interpersonal and competitive terms. For example, some naval aviators perceive their sole purpose in life to be to prepare themselves for the ultimate confrontation with an enemy (Derr, 1986). In that confrontation, these "warriors" would prove to themselves and to the world their superiority in competitive combat. Although the military version of this anchor may seem somewhat over-dramatized, other people in many other occupations also define life in such competitive terms. Many salespeople, professional athletes, and even some general managers and entrepreneurs define their careers essentially as daily combat or competition in which winning is everything.

Most people seek a certain level of challenge, but for the person anchored in pure challenge, it is the one thing that matters most. The area of work, the kind of employing organization, the pay system, the type of promotion system, and the forms of recognition are all subordinate to whether or not the job provides constant opportunities for self-tests. In the absence of such constant tests of self, the person becomes bored and irritable. Often such people talk about the importance of variety in their careers, and one reason some of them are attracted to general management is the variety and intense challenge that managerial situations can provide.

People anchored in pure challenge can also be very single-minded and certainly can make life difficult for those who do not have comparable aspirations. The 1979 Hollywood film *The Great Santini* depicted the problems created by a "warrior," both for his supervisors and for his family because there were no wars to be fought. A career for such a person has meaning only if competitive skills can be exercised; if there is no such opportunity, the person can become demoralized and hence a problem to him- or herself and others.

Type of work desired, pay and benefits, career growth, and forms of recognition will vary immensely in this group as a function of the actual kind of work they are doing. We need only compare the variation in these factors among "warriors," professional athletes, bond salesmen, some scientists, and engineers working on unsolved problems to see that there are no easy generalizations for this group, as is also the case for the next group.

Lifestyle

At first glance, this concept seems like a contradiction in terms. People who organize their existence around lifestyle are, in one sense, saying that their careers are less important to them and, therefore, that they do not have a career anchor. These people belong in a discussion of career anchors, however, because a growing number of people who are highly motivated toward meaningful careers are, at the same time, finding themselves in situations in which their careers must be integrated with their total lifestyles.

This situation has arisen for more and more people because of changing social values around independence; the growing number of women in full careers, which has led to many more dual-career families; the changing attitudes of employers toward giving less job security and more portability in benefits; and the growing number of families who cannot survive economically unless both spouses work. If people are told to manage their own careers and they have spouses with careers, it is inevitable that more and more people would think about designing their total life situation, not just their work (Bailyn, 1978, 1993).

Balancing personal and professional lives has always been an issue, but in a single-career family, a common resolution was and continues to be that one or the other spouse's career dominates and the other one becomes supportive. If two full careers are involved, the balancing process is much more complex, requiring economic, geographical, and other lifestyle decisions such as whether or not or when to have children and where to live.

Preferred Type of Work, Pay, and Benefits

An integration of career and lifestyle issues is itself an evolving process. Hence people who find themselves in this situation want flexibility more than anything else. Unlike the autonomy-anchored, who also want flexibility, those with lifestyle anchors are quite willing to work for organizations, do a variety of kinds of work, and accept organizational rules and restrictions, provided that the right options are available at the right time. Such options might include less travel or moving only at times when family situations permit, part-time work if life concerns require it, sabbaticals, paternity and maternity leaves, day-care options (which are becoming especially relevant for the growing population of dual-career couples and single parents), flexible working hours, work at home during normal working hours, and so on.

Lifestyle-anchored people look more for an organizational attitude than a specific program, an attitude that reflects respect for personal and family concerns and that makes genuine renegotiation of the work contract possible. People with this anchor require understanding and flexibility from their organizations and formal personnel policies that acknowledge the reality of the lifestyle issues. At any given time, it is not clear what particular organizational responses will be most helpful, except that policies and career systems in general must become more flexible and provide choices.

One specific lifestyle issue is the growing unwillingness of career occupants to move geographically, a move that is often associated with promotion. In the past, this seemed to be an aspect of the security/stability anchor, but it has become increasingly clear that people who are unwilling to move feel this way less for security/stability reasons than for reasons of wanting to integrate personal, family, and career issues. Moving two careers or moving kids out of a desired school at a critical age is something that many people are less and less willing to do, even if it costs them a promotion or some other desired career outcome.

This trend, if it continues, could have major implications for external career paths. Many companies take it for granted that people will move when asked to do so and treat this as a positive developmental career step. If they encounter more and more people anchored in lifestyle, it is not clear whether these people will have to sacrifice career advancement or whether their companies will have to redefine career paths to make advancement more feasible within a confined geographical area.

For example, the president of a large multinational company learned that one of his most likely successors did not want to leave a particular geographic area because of his wife's career and the desire to keep his kids in a given school. The president knew that this person needed international experience to continue his career growth and made it clear that if the person did not take the international assignment he would be off the promotional ladder for CEO. The person then had to choose, which meant deciding whether his anchor was general management or lifestyle.

If you find yourself in a situation in which the lifestyle anchor most nearly fits you, you need to look at what other career issues are important for you and determine how to build a lifestyle around those other career concerns.

Review of Questionnaire Scores

Now that you know what each anchor category refers to, go back to the *Career Anchors Self-Assessment* and look up your scores to see which anchor categories produced the highest and lowest scores. It is often useful to look first at the lowest scores to see what kinds of things *you do not care about.* Do you agree that these are unimportant areas for you? If not, go back and review some of the items that you gave low numbers to and ask yourself why you rated them the way you did.

Now look at the categories that produced the highest scores. Can you identify the one thing you would not give up, if forced to make a choice? Many people find at this point that there are two or three anchor categories that are high. This is normal because the questionnaire did not force you to make choices between categories. Again, the first step to further clarification is to look back at the items and see whether you would still rate them the same way. Many people find that they still have two or three categories that seem equally important. At this point you are ready to proceed to the next section to analyze your career *history*, either by yourself or preferably with the help of a partner who will interview you.

Identifying Career Anchors Through Career History Analysis

AN ANALYSIS OF YOUR PAST EDUCATIONAL and occupational decisions is ultimately the most reliable way to determine your career anchor. The *Career Anchors Self-Assessment* gives you a good picture of some of the things you care about, but your past decisions and the reasons for those decisions are an even deeper basis for self-insight. You can do the history yourself by writing out your answers to the questions on pages 28 through 33, but it often works better to have a partner interview you and help you decipher your own pattern of choices.

Choose a partner with whom you will feel free to share the events of your career so far, as well as your future aspirations. For this reason, it is best to avoid a superior or subordinate or a peer with whom you may be in competition. Your partner does not have to be the same age you are or be in the same line of work. Many people report that a spouse or a close friend makes a good partner.

The partner does not have to have any training as an interviewer; all of the questions to be asked are provided in this booklet. All that is needed is some interest and willingness to discuss your career with you.

The interview should take about one hour. Give this workbook to your partner so that he or she can take notes on the interview pages before returning it to you. For each decision, try to figure out *why* you made that decision. The anchor that will reveal itself gradually will show up best in the pattern of answers to the "why's." Chances are that, even if you have moved many times, there will be a pattern to the reasons why you moved. The interview will reveal that pattern.

Career Planning Interview Questions

Education

Let's start with your education. Where did you go to high school and college? What was the reason for each choice?

What did you major in? Why?

Did you go to graduate school? Where? Why?

What was your area of concentration? Why?

First Job

What was your first real job out of school? What were you looking for in this job? Why did you make the choice you made?

What were your long-range ambitions and goals as you started your career?

How did the first job work out in terms of your goals?

What were the most important things you learned on your first job?

Next Job

When and why did you make your first job/career change? What brought this about? Why did you move?

How did this job work out in terms of your goals?

What were the most important things you learned on this job?

What was the next job change or life event? Why did it occur?

(*Interviewer:* Ask the same set of questions about each change in jobs, organizations, or life circumstances. Use additional pieces of paper if necessary.)

Review

As you look back on your career so far, do you see any major turning points? What were they and why did they occur?

What were some things you especially enjoyed in your career so far? Why?

What were some things that you did not enjoy and would like to avoid in the future? Why?

In what way have your ambitions or career goals changed? What do you now see as your long-range goals?

What is the ideal final career goal or ultimate job you would like to have?

In describing yourself to others, how do you identify your work?

What do you see to be your major competencies?

What are some critical values that guide your choice of jobs and organizations?

Do you see any pattern in your career?

Reconciling the Self-Assessment Scores with the History Review

You should now compare what the quantitative score on the self-assessment reveals with what you learned in analyzing your history. If there are inconsistencies, try to figure out which is more valid—what you said on the self-assessment or the reasons you gave for your various career decisions. If you are working with a partner, he or she can help you to clarify what may be going on if there are inconsistencies.

Common Questions

As you have gone through this analysis, several other questions will have arisen in your mind. Some of the most common are reviewed below.

Are There Other Career Anchors?

Research to date indicates that most people can be described in terms of the eight anchors presented. These anchors have been found in a variety of occupations and apply equally well to doctors, lawyers, teachers, naval officers, consultants, police officers, and even production workers (if they are observed off the job). Even "nonpaying" occupations such as homemaking can be seen in terms of the different anchors; spouses of career-involved people find that they enjoy homemaking for reasons that mirror the anchor categories.

People often ask whether there are other anchors, especially ones centered around power, variety, pure creativity, or organizational identity. According to the research guideline used, if two or more cases absolutely did not fit the existing eight categories and clearly resembled each other in some dimension, an additional anchor category would be created. Thus far, each proposed dimension has proven to be an aspect of another anchor or has been expressed differently in different anchor groups.

Power and creativity, for example, seem to be universal needs that are expressed in different ways by different anchor groups. The technical/functional person expresses power through superior knowledge and skill; the entrepreneur through building an organization; the general manager through obtaining a position that provides rank, influence, and resources; the service-oriented person through moral persuasion; and so on. Similarly, creativity can be displayed in each of the anchor categories in different ways. Variety is something else that many people want and thrive on, but it is not an anchor per se because it can be obtained through autonomy, managerial challenges, entrepreneurial activity, or lifestyle. Only those anchored in technical/functional competence, security, and service trade some aspects of variety for other important considerations in their career evolutions.

From the point of view of this exercise in self-analysis, you should attempt to locate your "true" anchor, but you should also allow for the possibility that your pattern of competencies, motives, and values is unique. What is important is to get some insight into yourself so that you make better career choices in the future. The eight anchor categories should help you in this, but it is not necessary to force yourself to fit into one of them. What you must find out about yourself is what you would not give up if forced to make a choice. That is your true career anchor.

Can a Person Have More Than One Anchor?

A career anchor is defined as *the one thing a person would not give up if forced to make a choice.* This definition allows for only one anchor—the one set of talents, values, and motives at the top of one's personal hierarchy. However, many career situations make it possible to fulfill several sets of talents, motives, and values, making a choice unnecessary and thus preventing a person from finding out what is really at the top of his or her hierarchy. For example, a functional manager in a paternalistic company simultaneously can fulfill security, autonomy, technical/functional, managerial, and even lifestyle anchors. In order to determine an anchor, that person must then invent hypothetical career options that would force a choice. For example, would that person choose to be a division general manager or the chief corporate officer in his or her function? Most people can identify their true anchors if they pose such choice situations to themselves.

If no anchor emerges clearly for you, another possibility is that you have not had enough life experience to develop priorities that determine how to make those choices. If you are in this situation, you would benefit from determining what anchors are highest and should explore your reactions to different situations through systematic job choices. For example, if you do not know whether you have a talent or taste for general management and have had no opportunities in that area, you might volunteer to run a project, become a committee chairperson, ask to be acting manager of a unit, or try to gain experience in some other way. In lieu of this, you might find people who are clearly in that kind of job situation and interview them in detail about what it is like to be in that situation.

Do Anchors Change?

All the evidence is not in yet as to whether or not anchors change. Too few people have been studied for long enough periods of time to determine how career anchors evolve. However, many of the original panelists in this research have been followed into their mid-forties and fifties, and thus far, the weight of evidence is on the side of stability. One would expect this because, as people clarify their self-images—as they become more aware of what they are good at, want, and value—they tend to want to hold on to those self-images. The better people know themselves, the more they want to hold on to those insights.

For example, a technically/functionally anchored engineering manager in a large corporation found himself moving toward general management because of the nature of the external career path. Because he sensed that his next promotion would be to a generalist job, he began to lobby among his friends in senior management to be assigned to a high-level staff job at headquarters, and he successfully created this lateral move. He was willing to give up a promotion to a higher-level general-management job to remain in his preferred technical area.

Another technical/functional manager resigned because his job was boring to him and he was dead-ended. He then picked up his career as a successful consultant in that same technical/functional area. His career changed, but his anchor did not.

An autonomy-anchored individual dropped out of organizational life altogether and lived a marginal life until he married and had children. Instead of returning to the mainstream, he and his wife opened an antique shop that permitted him to remain autonomous.

Some people who make dramatic mid-life changes in their external careers are trying to actualize what were their anchors all along; they simply never had the chance to do what they really wanted to do. For example, a computer consultant with a technical/functional anchor who had always wanted to go to law school finally did so when a small inheritance enabled him to finance it. Following graduation, he drifted into small-town law and developed a successful practice using many of the computer and consulting skills he had acquired. He remained anchored in the technical/functional area.

Because of the way that careers are structured, one's job and one's career anchor often do not match. A technically/functionally anchored person might be promoted to general manager, or a managerially anchored person might be given a high-level staff job. A security-anchored person might be convinced to join an entrepreneurial venture, or an autonomy-oriented person might take a boring but stable job under a repressive boss to earn money. People are able to perform somewhat in such situations, but they are not happy and do not feel that their real selves are engaged. They can adapt to circumstances and make the best of them, but their anchors do not change; as soon as there is an opportunity, they will seek a better match.

You now should have a fairly clear idea of what your career anchor is. If you have experienced change in your own career, ask yourself whether the anchor changed or only the concerns that were occupying you at different career and life changes.

The next portion of this booklet is designed to help you decide whether your anchor and present career are a good match and, if not, how to think about future job possibilities.

Job/Role Analysis

THE PRIMARY FOCUS UP TO NOW has been on your own career history and the self-insights you have had about your competencies, your career motives, and the values that you hold strongly. The concept of career anchor captures these insights. But what are you to do next in a world in which more and more you are expected to take charge of your own career? To make intelligent plans, you need a vehicle to analyze present and future job situations, a process to enable you to decide whether to stay where you are, whether to try to move to a different organization in a different locale, and what forces are out there in the environment that you need to take account of.

In its simplest form, job/role analysis is a process of identifying the major stakeholders of a given job to create for yourself a "role map" that enables you to assess how well your job and your anchor fit with each other. If the fit is poor and you decide you need some career development moves, the job/role planning process enables you to create role maps of potential future jobs, along with some analysis of how the expectations of stakeholders will change as you look ahead and a self-assessment of the competencies you may need in those future jobs.

Analyzing Your Present Job

The analysis of your present job can be done by yourself by identifying the stakeholders and role senders of your present job. You will create a picture of your "role network," which is all of the people who have some expectations of you. The key stakeholders are those members of the role network whose own work will be severely affected if you do not meet their expectations.

Step 1. Create a Role Map

A job is a set of activities that relate you to various other people who have expectations of you. The first step in this job/role analysis is to identify who those others are and to create a visual overview of the network of people who are connected to you. This picture is your "Role Map" (see Figure 2).

Figure 2. Sample Role Map

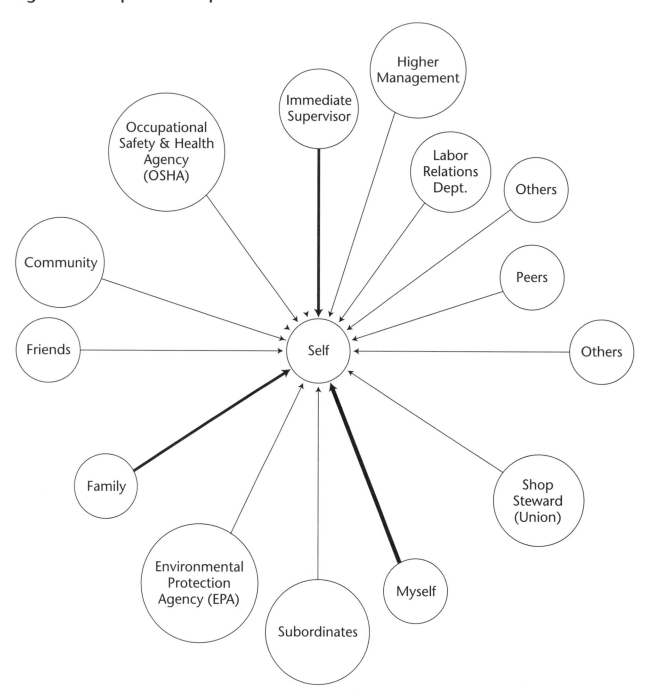

a. Using the blank page that follows these instructions, put yourself into the center.

b. If you are in an organization, put your boss near the top of the paper and draw an arrow toward yourself in the center.

c. Put your subordinates below you and draw an arrow from each of them toward you in the center.

d. Continue this process by writing down above, below, to the right, and to the left all of the people you can think of who expect something of you in your role. For example, peers in your organization, customers, members of the community, family members, friends, and any others. The purpose is to locate *all* of the people in your "role set" so that you can analyze all of the role expectations to which you have to respond. The width of the various arrows can represent the strength of the relationships.

e. Draw an arrow from yourself back to yourself because you also have expectations of how you plan to perform your job and what you expect of yourself in your job/role.

My Role Map

Step 2. List Major Role Sender Expectations

Once you have identified all of the people in your role set, make some notes in the space provided as to what the *major expectations are of each of the role senders,* especially the key role stakeholders such as your boss, peers, and subordinates. Try to identify the most essential role expectations, the things that are critical to the performance of your job/role.

Step 3. Identify Role Issues and Action Steps

Identifying stakeholder expectations will have likely revealed three important issues around roles—ambiguity, overload, and conflict—each of which is described below. Following each description is space for you to record your assessment of the situation and what you might do about it.

Role Ambiguity

For some role senders, you will not be sure what they expect of you. Consider what you might do to clarify their expectations and put those actions on your "to do" list. For example, you might ask for a meeting to discuss your understanding of your role and invite the role sender to discuss what he or she expects.

Role Overload

The sum total of what everyone expects of you will be much more than you can possibly do. How do you set priorities? Ask yourself whose expectations are most often responded to and whose are most often ignored? Do you communicate your own sense of priorities? For example, you might explicitly communicate to some role senders that you will be late or unable to do what they expect. If you can think of other ways of coping with overload, put the action steps on your "to do" list.

Role Conflict

You will discover that what some members of the role set expect is in direct conflict with what others expect or what you expect of yourself. Ask yourself how to resolve those conflicts, whether to deny that they exist, compromise by doing a little for each, confront the role sender? Think of action steps you can take to reduce the role conflicts and put those on your "to do" list. For example, if two of your peers expect things of you that are in conflict, consider bringing them together to examine what they expect and how that impacts you.

How Well Is Your Career Anchor Matched to Your Present Job?

Compare what you are looking for in terms of your career with what you have learned about your job and your role network. Are there major mismatches between your current job and what you are really looking for in terms of career and life style? If so, you are ready to use role maps to assess possible future kinds of work and, most importantly, to assess your readiness for new kinds of work challenges that are brought about by changes in the way work will be done in the future.

Analyzing Possible Future Jobs

In preparation for job/role planning, the next few pages outline some of the major changes that have occurred in the world of work and make some cautious predictions about how organizations and the world of work will change in the future. After you have read these pages, proceed to do your own job/role planning for possible future jobs (pages 51 through 52) and, on that basis, make concrete plans for your own career development.

1. *Organizations worldwide are continuing to reexamine their structures and are engaging in various kinds of "downsizing," "rightsizing," joint ventures, acquisitions, and mergers.* In order to remain competitive in an increasingly global world, organizations are discovering the need to be concerned about perpetual improvement, innovation, and stringent control of their costs. This has led to a wave of layoffs and restructuring of organizations such that many of the jobs have simply disappeared and work has been reallocated and redesigned so that a smaller number of people could perform it. The possibilities inherent in the creative use of information technology, especially "groupware," have opened up new ways of thinking about work and jobs. The ways in which people will be connected to each other will vary and will require all kinds of new relationships.

2. *Globalization and new technologies have loosened the boundaries of organizations, jobs, and roles.* At the organizational level, we see in many industries a loosening of the boundaries between suppliers, manufacturers, and customers. By using sophisticated information-technology tools, customers can directly access a company's sales organization, specify in detail what kind of product or service they require, and obtain an immediate price and delivery date from the computer. As such systems become more common, not only do the roles of purchasing agent and salesperson become much more ambiguous, but their role changes create a chain reaction throughout the organization requiring redefinition of order processing, marketing, and even design and manufacturing.

At the same time, the automation of everything from secretarial work to complex production processes makes all kinds of jobs from secretary to production worker much less manual and more conceptual. Operators who work in automated refineries, nuclear plants, paper mills, and other such organizations know as much about the running of the plant as the managers do, thereby creating new power relationships. The role of management becomes more ambiguous as managers no longer have the power of knowing things that their subordinates do not know. It is especially important for managers to discover that their relationships to their production workers have fundamentally changed, and that workers have come to occupy a much more central position in the role network.

3. *As work becomes technically more complex, fewer people will work in operational roles and more people will work in knowledge-based service and staff roles supporting the operation.* The goal of automation is generally to reduce headcount, but the result is typically more of a redistribution of workers. Fewer operators are needed, but more support services are required. The total cost of the operation ultimately may not change all that much, but the kinds of work that are performed change radically. The relationships between sets of workers will therefore change in as yet unknown ways. Operators have greater immediate responsibility for doing things right, but the programmers, systems engineers, and maintenance engineers have greater ultimate responsibility to keep the systems running, to keep the computers from "going

down." Management becomes more of a coordinating and liaison function and less of a monitoring and control function. Peers in service roles come to be seen as much more central in the role network than they had been previously.

4. *As conceptual work increases and job/role boundaries loosen, anxiety levels will increase.* The human organism depends on certain levels of predictability and stability in its environment. Although we all have needs for creativity and stimulation, we forget that those motives operate against a background of security, stability, and predictability. As organizations face increasing competitive pressures, as jobs become more conceptual, and as responsibility levels in all jobs increase, we will see stress and anxiety levels increase at all levels of the organization. Formalization and bureaucracy have been a defense against such anxiety, but the kind of work that needs to be done in the information and knowledge age requires more flexibility and innovation, thus making more anxiety an inevitable result.

An increasing role for management will be the containment and working through of anxiety levels, although it is not at all clear by what individual or group mechanisms this will occur. When people are anxious, they want to be with others, and one of the most important functions of groups in organizations is the management of shared anxiety. The increasing emphasis on groups and teams that we hear about continually may be the result not only of the growing complexity of work, but of the growing anxiety levels attending work.

The concept of sociotechnical systems has been promulgated for many decades, but as we project ahead, it would appear that it becomes a more important concept than ever. One cannot separate the technical elements of a job from the social elements.

5. *In the process of "rightsizing," organizations are (a) re-examining their hierarchical structures, (b) moving toward flatter organizations, (c) relying more on coordination mechanisms other than hierarchy, and (d) "empowering" their employees in various ways.* In the flat, networked, project-based organization of the future, power and authority will rotate among different project leaders, and individual project members will have to coordinate their own activities across a number of projects with different leaders. Operational authority will shift rapidly from one project leader to another, and individual employees may find themselves matrixed between several bosses simultaneously. At the same time, as knowledge and information are more widely distributed, employees will become de facto empowered, because increasingly they will know things that their bosses will not know.

However, hierarchy is fairly intrinsic to human systems, so we will probably not see the abandonment of hierarchical structures so much as a change in their function. In particular, the coordination of powerful project groups, divisions, and other organizational units will continue to require effective leadership and hierarchy to avoid the inevitable political power struggles that arise in an intergroup and inter-organizational context. For example, broad hierarchical categories such as civil service grades or degrees of partnership in a law firm or levels of professorial rank may continue to serve broad career-advancement functions, but may not be a good guide as to who will have operational authority over a given task or project. Respect for people and the amount of influence they exert will have more to do with their operational performance than with their formal rank, and hierarchy will increasingly be viewed as a necessary adjunct to organizational life rather than its prime principle.

Power and authority will derive from what a given person knows and what skills he or she has demonstrated. But since conceptual knowledge is largely invisible, the opportunities for misperception or conflicting perception of who knows what and who should be respected for what will increase, making the exercise of authority and influence much more problematic. This in turn will increase anxiety levels in organizations.

6. *Organizations are becoming more differentiated and complex.* With the rapid growth of technology in all fields of endeavor, the number of products and services available is increasing. At the same time, growing affluence and more widely distributed information about products and services are making consumers more demanding. Organizations are therefore having to respond by becoming more able to deliver more different kinds of products and services faster, in greater variety, and in more different places all over the globe.

One of the major consequences is that the organizations that make these products and/or deliver the services themselves have to be more differentiated and complex. That, in turn, means that there will be more different kinds of occupational specialists who must be managed and whose efforts must somehow be tied together into a coherent organizational whole. Many of these specialists are neither motivated nor able to talk to one another, creating special problems of integration of effort. The highly specialized design engineer or computer programmer working in the research and development end of the company or in manufacturing often has little in common with the financial analyst whose specialty is the management of the company's investment portfolio or the personnel specialist concerned with the most recent interpretation of the affirmative action legislation. Yet all of these and many other specialists contribute in major ways to the welfare of the total organization, and their efforts have to be integrated. Such integration cannot take place unless all of the specialists and managers involved become conscious of each other as stakeholders and begin to make an effort to respond to each other's expectations.

Beyond this, senior management must begin to worry about and plan for the specific career development of such specialists, in that many of them would be neither able nor willing to go into managerial positions. Such developmental planning cannot occur without a clear understanding of the role network within which these specialists operate and the involvement of those employees in planning their own development.

7. *The subunits of organizations develop subcultures that will have increasing difficulty in communicating with each other, in spite of the fact that they are increasingly interdependent.* In order to produce a complex product or service effectively over a period of

time, the many subspecialties of the organization will have to be coordinated and integrated, because they are simultaneously and sequentially interdependent in a variety of ways. For example, if the financial department does not manage the company's cash supply adequately, there is less opportunity for capital expansion or R&D; on the other hand, if an engineering design sacrifices some elements of quality for low cost, the result may be customer complaints, a lowered company reputation, and a subsequent decreased ability of the company to borrow money for capital expansion. In this sense, engineering and finance are in fact highly interdependent, even though each may be highly specialized and neither may interact with the other directly.

Sequential interdependence is the more common situation. The engineering department cannot design a product or service if R&D has not done a good job of developing the concept or prototype; in turn, manufacturing cannot build the product if engineering has produced unbuildable designs; and sales and marketing cannot do their jobs if they have poor products to sell. But, of course, R&D cannot get its concepts right if marketing has not given them clear pictures of future customer needs or possibilities, and the process innovations that occur within manufacturing often influence both marketing and engineering in terms of the types of products that are thought to be conceivable and feasible.

These types of interdependence have always existed within organizations. But as specialization increases, interdependence also increases, because the final product or service is more complex and more vulnerable to any of its parts malfunctioning. Nowhere is this clearer than in computer products or services. The hardware and software have to be designed properly in the first place and then implemented by a variety of specialists, who serve as the interface between the final user and the computer system. If any of the specialists fails to do his or her job, the entire service or product may fail.

Each specialty develops its own subculture—specialized jargon, certain ways of perceiving the world and analyzing problems, more responsiveness to the technical community than general management. Leadership and management de facto become a process of helping these subcultures to better understand each other and align themselves around organizational goals rather that their own subgoals.

8. *Organizational climates are becoming more collaborative/cooperative.* One major effect of the recognition of increased interdependence is that competition between organizational units or individuals is increasingly being perceived as potentially destructive. Teamwork and collaborative/cooperative relations are increasingly being touted as necessary to do the job. This trend runs counter to the external marketplace philosophy that competition is a good thing—rather, collaboration and "team work" are increasingly seen to be necessary adaptations within organizations, even if *inter*-organizational relations continue to be competitive.

If this trend is worldwide, one will begin to see more evidence of inter-organizational collaboration as well, not for political reasons but for practical reasons of technological necessity. Increased levels of coordination will not be achieved by more centralized planning, as had been attempted in the socialist economies, but by more distribution of information and decentralization that will permit the various units to coordinate among themselves. However, for this self-managed coordination to occur, not only must information be widely available, but all of the actors in the system must be able to decipher their roles in it. The same information can be framed and interpreted in many different ways by different subcultures. For collaboration and cooperation to work, common frames of reference must be established, and that process will involve organizational members in much more intercultural, group, and team activities. Building shared frames of reference will increasingly become a primary task of leadership.

This trend poses a particular dilemma for managers whose own careers have developed in very dog-eat-dog, competitive environments and who simply do not have the interpersonal competence to redesign their organizational processes to be more supportive of collaborative relations and cross-cultural understanding.

Many managers pay lip service to "teamwork," but their day-to-day style sends clear signals of not really understanding or supporting the concept, with the predictable consequence that the "team" does not function as a team at all. Unfortunately, both the manager and the subordinates may draw the erroneous conclusion that it is the teamwork *concept* that is at fault, rather than locating the problem in their failure to *implement* the concept. Once they understand the nature of the network they are in and its many cultural components, they can do a better job of implementation. Thus, the very activity of job/role analysis and planning, when carried out in a team, becomes an important team-building function.

9. *Organizations are becoming more dependent on lateral communication channels.* Closely connected with the need for more collaborative teamwork is the need for information to flow laterally between technical specialists, rather than going through a hierarchy. For example, some companies are putting the R&D and marketing departments closer to each other geographically and stimulating direct contact between them, rather than having higher levels of management attempt to translate marketing issues for the R&D people. The customer, the salesperson, and the marketing specialist in a complex industry such as electronics all probably know more about the technical side of the business than the general manager does, and therefore they must be brought into direct interaction with the designer and engineer if a viable product or service is to result.

The information-processing needs of organizations based on task complexity and environmental uncertainty should, in fact, be the major determinants of organization structure. Multi-level hierarchical structures work only so long as task complexity and uncertainty are fairly low. Lateral structures, such as project teams, task forces, ad hoc committees, cross-functional organizational units, and matrix management, become more common with increased complexity and uncertainty.

Technological possibilities and consumer demands are driving to greater complexity, and information technology will make it possible for organizations eventually to adapt by creating the kinds of lateral communication that will make coordination, integration, and genuine teamwork possible.

Here again, managers face a novel situation because of the likelihood that their own careers have been spent in organizational settings dedicated to principles of hierarchy and chains of command. In such "traditional" organizations, the tendency to communicate with people outside the chain of command is actually discouraged and punished. Not only will the organizational reward system and climate have to shift to encourage lateral communication but, in addition, managers will have to be trained to create lateral structures and to make them work, taking into account that these groups will have different subcultures.

10. *Socio-cultural values around family, self, and work are changing.* People are placing less value on traditional concepts of organizational loyalty and the acceptance of authority based on formal position, age, or seniority and are placing more value on individualism and individual rights vis-a-vis the large organization. Increasingly, people are demanding that the tasks they are asked to perform make sense and provide them with some challenge and opportunity to express their talents. Increasingly, people are demanding that the rights of individuals be protected, especially if they are members of minority groups or are in danger of being discriminated against on some arbitrary basis, such as sex, age, religion, or ethnicity. Increasingly, people are demanding some voice in decisions that affect them, leading to the growth of various forms of "industrial democracy," participative management, and worker involvement in job design and corporate decision making.

As noted above, from the point of view of the employing organization, worker involvement also makes sense to the extent that the trend toward specialization of tasks is occurring. For many kinds of decisions, it is the worker who has the key items of information and therefore must be involved if the decision is to be a sound one. Thus, employee "empowerment" has taken on almost fad status.

People are placing less value on work or career as a total life concern and less value on promotion or hierarchical movement within the organization as the sole measure of "success" in life. Instead, more value is being placed on leading a balanced life in which work, career, family, and self-development all receive their fair share of attention, and "success" is increasingly being defined in terms of the full use of all one's talents and contributing not only to one's work organization, but to family, community, and self as well. Careers are built on different kinds of career anchors, and the measures of success and advancement vary with whether or not one is oriented around the managerial, technical/functional, security, autonomy, entrepreneurial, service, pure challenge, or lifestyle anchor.

People are placing less value on traditional concepts of male and female gender roles with respect to both work and family roles. Thus, in the career and work area, we are seeing a growing trend toward equal employment opportunities for men and women, a breaking down of gender-role stereotypes in regard to work (for example, more women are going into engineering and more men are going into nursing), and a similar breaking down of gender-role stereotypes in regard to the proper family roles (more women are becoming primary "breadwinners," and more men are staying home to take care of children, do the cooking, and clean the house). Our society is opening up the range of choices for both men and women to pursue new kinds of work, family roles, and lifestyles. One of the major consequences has been the "dual-career" family, in which both husband and wife are committed to career development, thus forcing organizations to develop new personnel policies and forcing social institutions to develop new alternatives for childcare.

People are placing less value on economic growth and are placing relatively more value on conserving and protecting the quality of the environment in which they live. Assessing the impact of technology is becoming a major activity in our society, and we see growing evidence of a willingness to stop "progress," for example, reluctance to build the supersonic transport or even allow our airports to use existing SSTs; highway construction that comes to an abrupt halt in the middle of a city; and refusal to build oil refineries or nuclear plants, even in economically depressed areas, if the environment would be endangered. However, as we have seen in the last two decades, if recessions occur or political climates shift, economic growth values resurface strongly, and conflict between the need to protect the environment and the need for jobs grows.

These value changes and conflicts have created a situation in which the incentives and rewards offered by the different parts of our society have become much more diverse, and consequently much less integrated. We see this most clearly in the organizational "generation gap"—older managers or employees who still operate from a "Protestant ethic" attitude toward work, versus young employees who question arbitrary authority, meaningless work, organization loyalty, restrictive personnel policies, and even fundamental corporate goals and prerogatives.

As options and choices have opened up and as managers have begun to question the traditional success ethic, they have become more ready to refuse promotions or geographical moves, more willing to "retire on the job" while pursuing family activities or off-the-job hobbies more actively, and have even resigned from high-potential careers to pursue various kinds of "second careers" seen to be more challenging and/or rewarding by criteria other than formal hierarchical position or amount of pay.

Job/Role Planning for Future Career Options

YOU MAY HAVE IN MIND SOME POSSIBLE future kinds of jobs. In order to determine whether such jobs might suit you and fit with your career anchor, you need to create role maps for such jobs. You may not have enough information to do this by yourself, so you must locate two or more people who are in those jobs or closely related jobs.

In considering future jobs, it is preferable to gather together two or three colleagues, peers, subordinates, or even supervisors, all of whom would be familiar with that future job.

Step 1: Use the blank page following these instructions and put the job in the center.

Step 2: With the help of your colleagues, draw a role map to identify the key stakeholders of that job.

Step 3: Analyze the expectations of the key stakeholders and, in particular, speculate on how those expectations will change as you look ahead, given some of the trends identified above.

Step 4: Rate yourself on the job competencies shown on pages 53–56.

Step 5: Determine whether there is a good fit between the way you analyzed the job, the competencies needed in that job, your self-rating on those competencies (see next section), and your career anchor.

Future Job Role Map

Self-Assessment of Future Job/Role Requirements

A FUTURE JOB MAY BE COMPATIBLE WITH YOUR CAREER ANCHOR, yet may require of you certain motives, competencies, and values that you lack, indicating developmental needs that you should address in the immediate future. To help you analyze yourself in that regard, below is a list of fifty such items on which you can rate yourself. You can then think about dimensions that a future job would require and determine to what degree you qualify on that dimension.

Instructions: Rate yourself on each of the items below. A "1" means you do not possess that motive, competence, or value to any degree, while a "4" means you possess it to a great degree. For each item, provide two ratings. Put a *circle* around the number that represents where you think you are now. Put a *cross* through the number where you think you ought to be, given your job/role planning analysis. Try to be honest with yourself because this is not a test but a way of identifying your own strengths and developmental needs.

A. Motives and Values

	Low			High
1. My desire to get a job done, my need for accomplishment	1	2	3	4
2. My commitment to my organization and its mission	1	2	3	4
3. My career aspirations and ambitions	1	2	3	4
4. My degree of involvement with my career	1	2	3	4
5. My desire for high levels of responsibility	1	2	3	4
6. My desire to take risks	1	2	3	4
7. My desire to make tough decisions	1	2	3	4
8. My desire to work with and through people	1	2	3	4

	Low			High
9. My desire to exercise power and authority	1	2	3	4
10. My desire to monitor and supervise the activities of others	1	2	3	4
11. My desire to delegate and help others to succeed	1	2	3	4
12. My desire to function as a general manager free of functional and technical constraints	1	2	3	4
13. My desire to work collaboratively rather than competitively with others	1	2	3	4
14. My desire to learn	1	2	3	4
15. My desire to take risks even if that leads to errors	1	2	3	4

B. Analytical Abilities and Skills

	Low			High
16. My ability to identify problems in complex, ambiguous situations	1	2	3	4
17. My ability to sense quickly what information is needed in relation to a complex problem	1	2	3	4
18. My ability to obtain needed information from others	1	2	3	4
19. My ability to assess the validity of information that I have not gathered myself	1	2	3	4
20. My ability to learn quickly from experience	1	2	3	4
21. My ability to detect errors in my own actions	1	2	3	4
22. My flexibility, my ability to think of and implement different solutions for different kinds of problems	1	2	3	4
23. My creativity, ingenuity	1	2	3	4
24. My breadth of perspective and insight into a wide variety of situations	1	2	3	4
25. My degree of insight into myself (strengths and weaknesses)	1	2	3	4

C. Interpersonal and Group Skills

	Low			High
26. My ability to develop open and trusting relationships with peers	1	2	3	4

	Low			High
27. My ability to develop open and trusting relationships with superiors	1	2	3	4
28. My ability to develop open and trusting relationships with subordinates	1	2	3	4
29. My ability to listen to others in an understanding way	1	2	3	4
30. My ability to communicate my own thoughts and ideas clearly and persuasively	1	2	3	4
31. My ability to communicate my feelings clearly	1	2	3	4
32. My ability to influence people over whom I have no direct control	1	2	3	4
33. My ability to influence my peers	1	2	3	4
34. My ability to influence my superiors	1	2	3	4
35. My ability to influence my subordinates	1	2	3	4
36. My ability to diagnose complex interpersonal and group situations	1	2	3	4
37. My ability to develop processes that ensure high-quality decisions without having to make the decision myself	1	2	3	4
38. My ability to develop a climate of collaboration and teamwork	1	2	3	4
39. My ability to design processes to facilitate intergroup and inter-functional coordination	1	2	3	4
40. My ability to create a climate of growth and development for my subordinates	1	2	3	4

D. Emotional Abilities and Skills

	Low			High
41. The degree to which I am able to make up my own mind without relying on the opinions of others	1	2	3	4
42. The degree to which I am able to share power with others	1	2	3	4
43. The degree to which I am able to tolerate and acknowledge errors	1	2	3	4

	Low			High
44. My degree of tolerance for ambiguity and uncertainty	1	2	3	4
45. My ability to take risks, to pursue a course of action even if it may produce negative consequences	1	2	3	4
46. My ability to pursue a course of action even if it makes me anxious and uncomfortable	1	2	3	4
47. My ability to confront and work through conflict situations (versus suppressing or avoiding them)	1	2	3	4
48. My ability to keep going after an experience of failure	1	2	3	4
49. My ability to confront my stakeholders if there is role ambiguity, overload, or conflict	1	2	3	4
50. My ability to continue to function in the face of continued environmental turbulence	1	2	3	4

List below other items that occur to you

Developmental Implications and Next Steps

FIRST LOOK AT THOSE ITEMS FROM THE SELF-ASSESSMENT you just took where there is the greatest discrepancy between your present rating and where you feel you should be. For each area for which you feel there is a significant discrepancy, figure out a development plan for yourself or figure out how to restructure your job so that your present capacity will be sufficient to do the job.

If you conclude that you must restructure your job, think that through in terms of renegotiating with the requisite stakeholders and ensure that the new expectations are realistic, both from your point of view and their points of view.

List below the various developmental or restructuring actions you plan to take and keep this list as a point of reference to be reviewed at various times.

Item Number: _____

Developmental Plan:

Item Number: _____

Developmental Plan:

Item Number: _____

Developmental Plan:

Item Number: _____

Developmental Plan:

Item Number: _____

Developmental Plan:

Given all of the plans you've made, what are the next steps that you will take? Try to be specific and give a time frame for each step.

Step 1:

Time Table:

Step 2:

Time Table:

In conclusion, your own career development will depend on your ability to know yourself and to decipher the requirements of future jobs and career options. Think especially of how your career anchor, what you value and do not wish to give up, matches with the possibilities and constraints of the role networks of future jobs. You will find that periodically revisiting the self-assessment, the career history, and the role-mapping exercise will allow you to reflect and to make better career and life decisions.

References and Additional Resources

Arthur, M.B. & Rousseau, D.M. (Eds.) (1996). *The boundaryless career.* New York: Oxford.

Bailyn, L. (1978). Accommodation of work to family. In R. Rapoport & R.N. Rapoport (Eds.), *Working couples.* New York: Harper & Row.

Bailyn, L. (1992). Changing the conditions of work: Implications for career development. In D.H. Montross & C.J. Schinkman (Eds.), *Career development in the 1990s: Theory and practice.* Springfield, IL: Thomas.

Bailyn, L. (1993). *Breaking the mold.* New York: The Free Press.

Bianchi, S.M., Casper, L.M., & King, R.B. (Eds.). (2005). *Work, family, health and well-being.* Mahwah, NJ: Erlbaum.

Davis, S.M., & Davidson, B. (1991). *2020 vision.* New York: Simon & Schuster.

Derr, C.B. (1986). *Managing the new careerists.* San Francisco: Jossey-Bass.

Durcan, J., & Oates, D. (1996). *Career paths for the 21st century.* London: Century Business Press.

Hall, D.T. (2002). *Careers in and out of organizations.* Thousand Oaks, CA: Sage.

Kossek, E., & Lambert, S. (Eds.). (2005). *Work and life integration: Cultural and individual perspectives.* Mahwah, NJ: Erlbaum.

Poelmans, S.A.Y. (Ed.). (2005). *Work and family: An international research perspective.* Mahwah, NJ: Erlbaum.

Schein, E.H. (1971). The individual, the organization, and the career: A conceptual scheme. *Journal of Applied Behavioral Science, 7,* 401-426.

Schein, E.H. (1975). How career anchors hold executives to their career paths. *Personnel, 52,* 11-24.

Schein, E.H. (1977). Career anchors and career paths: A panel study of management school graduates. In J. Van Maanen (Ed.), *Organizational careers: Some new perspectives.* Hoboken, NJ: John Wiley & Sons.

Schein, E.H. (1978). *Career dynamics: Matching individual and organizational needs.* Reading, MA: Addison-Wesley.

Schein, E.H. (1987). Individuals and careers. In J. Lorsch (Ed.), *Handbook of organizational behavior.* Englewood Cliffs, NJ: Prentice-Hall.

Schein, E.H. (2004). *Organizational culture and leadership* (3rd ed.). San Francisco: Jossey-Bass.

Notes

Notes

Notes